The Ultimate Self-Teaching Method! Level 1

LEACH LIBRARY
276 Mammoth Road
Londonderry, NH 03053
432-1132

02 Dec 27
Unique Books
1595

788.6
PLA

Play
Clarinet
Today!

A Complete
Guide to
the Basics

P9-CRW-109

ISBN 0-634-03329-8

HAL•LEONARD®
CORPORATION

7777 W. BLUEMOUND RD. P.O. BOX 13819 MILWAUKEE, WI 53213

Copyright © 2001 by HAL LEONARD CORPORATION
International Copyright Secured   All Rights Reserved

For all works contained herein:
Unauthorized copying, arranging, adapting, recording or public performance is an infringement of copyright.
Infringers are liable under law.

Visit Hal Leonard Online at
www.halleonard.com

1. Clarinet - method -
Self-instruction.

Introduction

Welcome to *Play Clarinet Today!*—the series designed to prepare
you for any style of clarinet playing, from rock to blues to jazz to
classical. Whatever your taste in music, *Play Clarinet Today!* will
give you the start you need.

About the CD

It's easy and fun to play clarinet, and the accompanying CD will
make your learning even more enjoyable, as we take you step by
step through each lesson and play each song along with a full
band. Much as a real lesson, the best way to learn this material is to
read and practice a while first on your own, then listen to the CD.
With *Play Clarinet Today!*, you can learn at your own pace. If there
is ever something that you don't quite understand the first time
through, go back on the CD and listen again. Every musical track
has been given a track number, so if you want to practice a song
again, you can find it right away.

Contents

The Basics

The Parts of the Clarinet

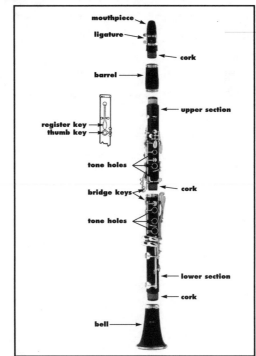

Posture

Whether sitting on the edge of your chair or standing, you should always keep your:

- Spine straight and tall,
- Shoulders back and relaxed, and
- Feet flat on the floor.

Breathing & Air Stream

Breathing is a natural thing we all do constantly, but you must control your breathing while playing the clarinet. To discover the correct air stream to play your clarinet:

- Place the palm of your hand near your mouth.
- Inhale deeply through the corners of your mouth, keeping your shoulders steady. Your waist should expand like a balloon.
- Whisper "too" as you gradually exhale a stream of air into your palm.

The air you feel is the air stream. It produces sound through the instrument. Your tongue is like a faucet or valve that releases or stops the air stream.

Your First Tone

Your mouth's position on the instrument is called the embouchure (ahm' bah shure). Developing a good embouchure takes time and effort, so carefully follow these beginning steps:

- First place the reed on the mouthpiece.

  Put the thin end of the reed in your mouth to moisten it thoroughly.

  Looking at the flat side of the mouthpiece, the ligature screws extend to your right. Slide the ligature up with your thumb.

  Place the flat side of the moist reed against the opening on the flat side of the mouthpiece. The thin tip of the reed should be almost even with the tip of the mouthpiece (only a hairline of the mouthpiece should be seen above the reed).

  While holding the reed in place with your left thumb, guide the ligature down over the mouthpiece and reed. (If your mouthpiece has two thin lines or grooves around it, position the ligature between these lines.)

  Gently tighten the screws on the ligature.

- Moisten your lips and roll the lower lip over your bottom teeth. A little of the red of the lower lip should be outside the teeth.

- Stretch your chin downward so it feels flat and pointed.

- Firming the corners of your mouth like a slightly puckered smile, place the mouthpiece about 1/2 inch into your mouth with the reed on your lower lip.

- Close your mouth around the mouthpiece with your upper teeth touching the top of the mouthpiece and your bottom teeth should gently apply pressure into your bottom lip so that your mouthpiece is being held firmly in place.

- The tip of your tongue should be behind your bottom teeth.

- Gently press your tongue forward, but keep the tip behind your bottom teeth. As you do this you will feel the reed touch your tongue about 1/2 inch back from the tip of the tongue so that no air could escape if you were to blow.

- Simultaneously blow into your instrument as you quickly pull your tongue back from the reed as if whispering "too."

- Keep your air moving at a steady rate of speed, and don't allow your cheeks to puff out as you blow. If you have trouble getting a clear sound, try putting more of the mouthpiece in your mouth. If you get a squeak you probably have too much mouthpiece in your mouth.

- This procedure for beginning a note is called "tonguing," and every note that you play should begin this way for the time being.

Reading Music

Musical sounds are indicated by symbols called **notes** written on a **staff**. Notes come in several forms, but every note indicates **pitch** and **rhythm**.

The Staff

Music Staff

Ledger Lines

The **music staff** has 5 lines and 4 spaces where notes and rests are written.

Ledger lines extend the music staff. Notes on ledger lines can be above or below the staff.

Measures & Bar Lines

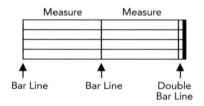

Measure   Measure

Bar Line   Bar Line   Double
                        Bar Line

Bar lines divide the music staff into **measures.**
The **Double Bar** indicates the end of a piece of music.

Treble Clef
(G Clef) indicates the position of note names on a music staff: Second line is G.

Time Signature
indicates how many beats per measure and what kind of note gets one beat.

= **4 beats** per measure
= **Quarter note** gets one beat

Pitch

Pitch (the highness or lowness of a note) is indicated by the horizontal placement of the note on the staff. Notes higher on the staff are higher in pitch; notes lower on the staff are lower in pitch. To name the pitches, we use the first seven letters of the alphabet: A, B, C, D, E, F, and G. The *treble clef* (𝄞) assigns a particular pitch name to each line and space on the staff, centered around the pitch G, located on the second line of the staff. Music for the clarinet is always written in the treble clef. (Some instruments may make use of other clefs, which make the lines and spaces represent different pitches.)

Note Names

Each note is on a line or space of the staff. These note names are indicated by the Treble Clef.

Sharps, Flats, and Naturals

These musical symbols are called accidentals which raise or lower the pitch of a note.

Sharp ♯ raises the note and remains in effect for the entire measure.

Flat ♭ lowers the note and remains in effect for the entire measure.

Natural ♮ cancels a flat (♭) or sharp (♯) and remains in effect for the entire measure.

Rhythm

Rhythm refers to how long, or for how many *beats* a note lasts. The beat is the pulse of music, and like your heartbeat it usually remains very steady. To help keep track of the beats in a piece of music, the staff is divided into *measures*. The *time signature* (numbers such as $\frac{4}{4}$ or $\frac{6}{8}$ at the beginning of the staff) indicates how many beats you will find in each measure. Counting the beats or tapping your foot can help to maintain a steady beat. Tap you foot down on each beat and up on each "&."

$\frac{4}{4}$ Time

Count:	1	&	2	&	3	&	4	&
Tap:	↓	↑	↓	↑	↓	↑	↓	↑

$\frac{4}{4}$ is probably the most common time signature. The **top number** tells you how many beats are in each measure; the **bottom number** tells you what kind of note receives one beat. In $\frac{4}{4}$ time there are four beats in the measure and a **quarter note** ($\downarrow$ or $\curlyvee$) equals one beat.

> **4** = **4 beats** per measure
> **4** = **Quarter note** gets one beat

Assembling Your Clarinet

- Put the thin end of the reed into your mouth to moisten it thoroughly while assembling your instrument. Occasionally rub a small amount of cork grease into the strips of cork around the mouthpiece and the upper and lower sections, then wipe the excess off the clarinet and your fingers.

- Hold the upper section in your left hand. Press your fingers over the tone holes. Take the lower section with your right hand and again press your fingers over the tone holes. Gently twist the two sections together so that the tone holes are aligned and the upper section's bridge key is directly over the lower section's bridge key. (Refer to the picture under "The Parts of the Clarinet.")

- Twist the bell onto the cork of the lower section, and twist the wider end of the barrel onto the cork of the upper section.

- Twist the mouthpiece into the barrel. The flat side of the mouthpiece should form a straight line with the register key on the upper section and the thumb rest on the lower section. Place the reed on the mouthpiece (see "Your First Tone" on page 5).

How to Hold Your Clarinet

- Hold the clarinet with your right thumb under the thumb rest. This thumb supports the weight of the clarinet. Be sure that the thumb rest touches your thumb just at the base of the thumbnail. Your left thumb should cover the thumb key. Cover the tone holes with the pads of your fingers, letting them curve naturally.

- When the clarinet is in your mouth, keep the bell at a 45° angle from your body. Hold the clarinet as shown:

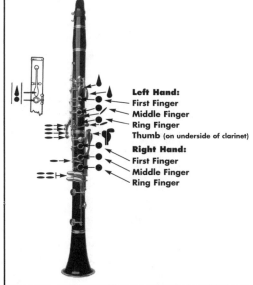

Left Hand:
First Finger
Middle Finger
Ring Finger
Thumb (on underside of clarinet)

Right Hand:
First Finger
Middle Finger
Ring Finger

Putting Away Your Instrument

- Remove the reed, wipe off excess moisture and return it to the reed case.

- Remove the mouthpiece and wipe the inside with a clean cloth. Once a week, wash the mouthpiece with warm tap water. Dry thoroughly.

- Hold the upper section with your left hand and the lower section with your right hand. Gently twist the sections apart. Shake out the excess moisture, then drop a weighted chamois or cotton swab into each section and pull it out the bottom.

- Carefully twist the barrel and the bell off each section. Dry off any additional moisture.

- As you put each piece back in the case, check to be sure they are dry.

- If your clarinet is made of wood, you will need to occasionally apply a special oil to the inside bore of the instrument to prevent cracking. You can get more information from your instrument dealer or from an experienced clarinetist.

Lesson 1

Track 1

The First Note: G

G is played "open" that is, with no keys pressed. Keep your fingers just above the tone holes, relaxed and curved.

Notes and Rests

Music uses symbols to indicated both the length of sound and of silence. Symbols indicating sound are called **Notes**. Symbols indicating silence are called **Rests**.

Whole Note/Whole Rest

A whole note means to play for four full beats (a complete measure in $\frac{4}{4}$ time). A whole rest means to be silent for four full beats.

Whole note	Half note	Quarter note	Eighth note
o	♩	♩	♪
Whole rest	Half rest	Quarter rest	Eighth rest
▬	▬	𝄽	𝄾

Listen to recorded track on the CD, then play along. Try to match the sound on the recording.

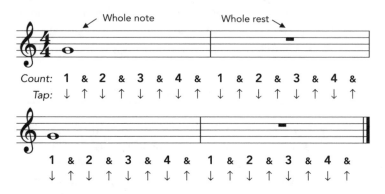

10

Count and Play

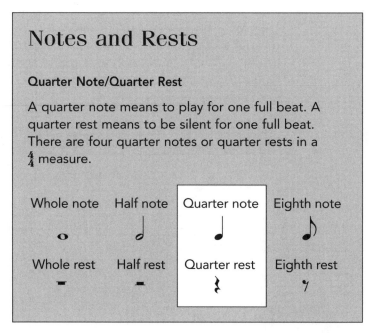

Notes and Rests

Quarter Note/Quarter Rest

A quarter note means to play for one full beat. A quarter rest means to be silent for one full beat. There are four quarter notes or quarter rests in a $\frac{4}{4}$ measure.

Whole note	Half note	Quarter note	Eighth note
o	𝅗𝅥	♩	♪
Whole rest	Half rest	Quarter rest	Eighth rest
▬	▬	𝄽	𝄾

Each note should begin with a quick "tu" to help separate it from the others.

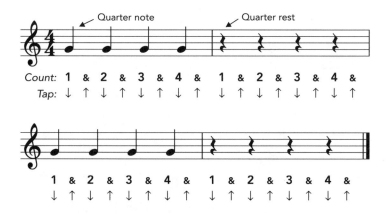

Don't just let the CD play on. Repeat each exercise until you feel comfortable playing it by yourself and with the CD.

Track 3

A New Note: F

Look for the fingering diagram under each new note. Press down the keys that are colored in. Practicing long tones like this will help to develop your sound and your breath control, so don't just move on to the next exercise. Repeat each one several times.

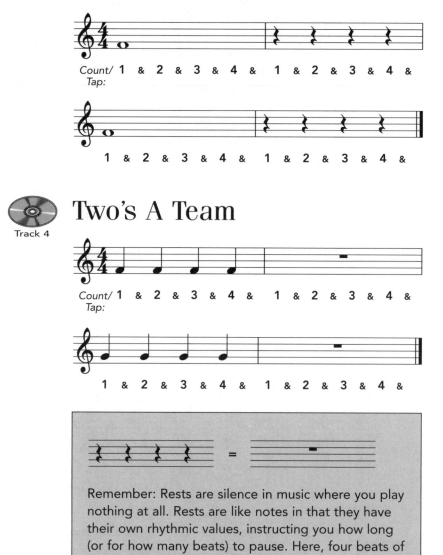

Count/ 1 & 2 & 3 & 4 & 1 & 2 & 3 & 4 &
Tap:

1 & 2 & 3 & 4 & 1 & 2 & 3 & 4 &

Track 4

Two's A Team

Count/ 1 & 2 & 3 & 4 & 1 & 2 & 3 & 4 &
Tap:

1 & 2 & 3 & 4 & 1 & 2 & 3 & 4 &

Remember: Rests are silence in music where you play nothing at all. Rests are like notes in that they have their own rhythmic values, instructing you how long (or for how many beats) to pause. Here, four beats of rest can be simplified as a whole rest.

A New Note: E

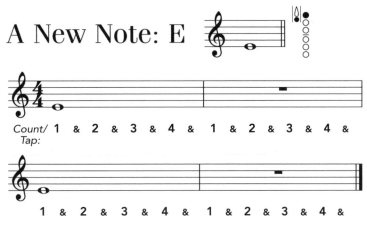

Count/
Tap: 1 & 2 & 3 & 4 &   1 & 2 & 3 & 4 &

1 & 2 & 3 & 4 &   1 & 2 & 3 & 4 &

Keeping Time

To keep a steady tempo, try tapping your foot
and counting along with each song. In $\frac{4}{4}$ time, tap
your foot four times in each measure and count,
"1 & 2 & 3 & 4 &." Your foot should touch the
floor on the number and come up on the "&."
Each number and each "&" should be exactly
the same duration, like the ticking of a clock.

Moving On Up

If you become winded or dizzy, you can still practice by
fingering the notes on your instrument and singing the
pitches or counting the rhythm out loud.

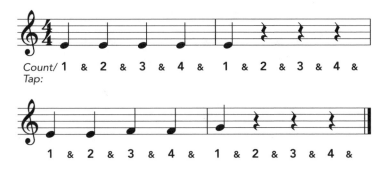

Count/
Tap: 1 & 2 & 3 & 4 &   1 & 2 & 3 & 4 &

1 & 2 & 3 & 4 &   1 & 2 & 3 & 4 &

A New Note: D

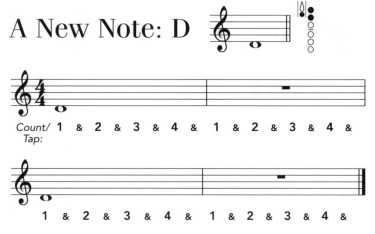

Count/ Tap: 1 & 2 & 3 & 4 & 1 & 2 & 3 & 4 &

1 & 2 & 3 & 4 & 1 & 2 & 3 & 4 &

Four By Four

Repeat Signs

Repeat signs ||: :|| tell you to repeat everything between them. If only the sign on the right appears (:||), repeat from the beginning of the piece.

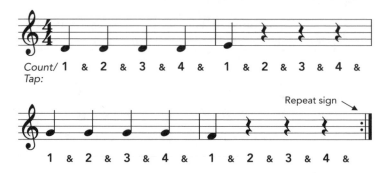

Count/ Tap: 1 & 2 & 3 & 4 & 1 & 2 & 3 & 4 &

Repeat sign

1 & 2 & 3 & 4 & 1 & 2 & 3 & 4 &

A New Note: C

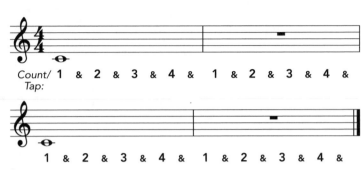

Count/ 1 & 2 & 3 & 4 & 1 & 2 & 3 & 4 &
Tap:

1 & 2 & 3 & 4 & 1 & 2 & 3 & 4 &

The Fab Five

1 & 2 & 3 & 4 & 1 & 2 & 3 & 4 &

1 & 2 & 3 & 4 & 1 & 2 & 3 & 4 &

First Flight

Keep the beat steady by silently counting or tapping while you play.

15

Rolling Along

Tonguing

To start each note, whisper the syllable "too." Keep the air stream going continuously. If the notes change, be sure to move your fingers quickly so that each note will come out cleanly. When you come to a rest or the end of the song, just stop blowing. Using your tongue to stop the air will cause an abrupt and unpleasant ending of the sound.

- Play long tones to warm up at the beginning of every practice session.
- Tap, count out loud and sing through each exercise with the CD before you play it.
- Play each exercise several times until you feel comfortable with it.

Track 13

Hot Cross Buns

Notes and Rests

Half Note/Half Rest

A half note means to play for two full beats. (It's equal in length to two quarter notes.) A half rest means to be silent for two beats. There are two half notes or half rests in a $\frac{4}{4}$ measure.

Whole note	Half note	Quarter note	Eighth note
o	𝅗𝅥	𝅘𝅥	𝅘𝅥𝅮
Whole rest	Half rest	Quarter rest	Eighth rest
▬	▬	𝄽	𝄾

Half note   Half rest

Go Tell Aunt Rhodie

Breath Mark

The breath mark (ʼ) indicates a specific place to inhale. Play the proceeding note for the full length then take a deep, quick breath through your mouth.

Make certain that your cheeks don't puff out when you blow.

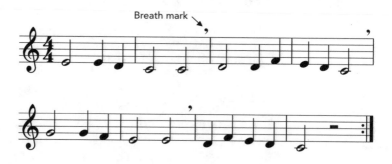

The Whole Thing

Remember: a whole rest (-) indicates a whole measure of silence. Note that the whole rest hangs down from the 4th line, whereas the half rest sits on the 3rd line.

Lightly Row

Reaching Higher
(New Note: A)

To play this new note, roll your finger of your left hand toward you and touch the A-key with the side of your finger. Always practice long tones on each new note.

Fermata

The fermata (𝄐) indicates that a note or rest is held somewhat longer than normal.

Fermata

Au Claire De La Lune

Twinkle, Twinkle Little Star

Check these points so you will get the best sound from your clarinet.

- Is your reed thoroughly moist, even the part that is against the mouthpiece?
- Are your fingers completely covering the tone holes?
- Are your top teeth resting firmly on the mouthpiece?

Track 20

Deep Pockets (New Note: B)

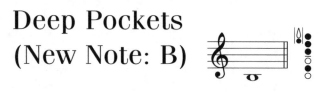

Always practice long tones on each new note.

Track 21

Doodle All Day

21

Breath Support

In order to play in tune and with a full, beautiful tone, it is necessary to breathe properly and control the air as you play. Quickly take the breath in through your mouth all the way to the bottom of your lungs. Then tighten your stomach muscles and push the air quickly through the clarinet, controlling the air with your lips. Practice this by forming your lips as you do when you play and then blowing against your hand. If the air is cool, you are doing it correctly. If the air is warm, tighten the lips and make the air stream smaller. Keep the air stream moving fast at all times, especially as you begin to run out of air. Practice blowing against your hand and see how long you can keep the air going. Work to keep the air stream cold and steady from beginning to end.

Now try this with your clarinet. Select a note that is comfortable to play and see how long you can hold it. Listen carefully to yourself to see if the tone gets louder or softer, changes pitch slightly, or if the quality of the tone changes. Do this a few times every time you practice, trying to hold the note a little longer each time and maintain a good sound.

Jingle Bells

Dynamics

Dynamics refer to how loud or soft the music is. Traditionally, many musical terms (including dynamic markings) are called by their Italian names:

f forte *(four' tay)*   loud

mf mezzo forte *(met' zoh four' tay)* moderately loud

p piano *(pee ahn' oh)*   soft

Producing a louder sound requires more air, but you should use full breath support at all dynamic levels.

Track 23

My Dreydl

Pick-up Notes

Sometimes there are notes that come before the first full measure. They are called *pick-up notes*. Often, when a song begins with a pick-up measure, the note's value (in beats) is subtracted from the last measure. To play this song with a one beat pick-up, you count "1, 2, 3" and start playing on beat 4.

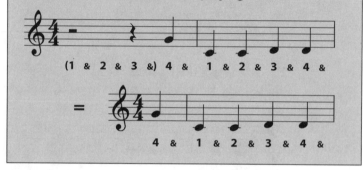

Last measure has 3 beats, not 4

24

Eighth Note Jam

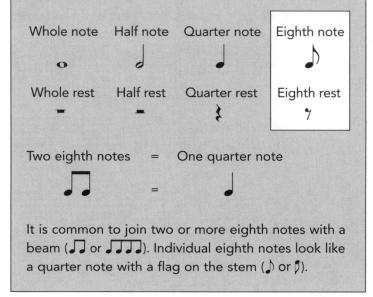

Notes and Rests

Eighth Note/Eighth Rest

An eighth note half the value of a quarter note, that is, half a beat. A eighth rest means to be silent for half a beat. There are eight eighth notes or eight eighth rests in a $\frac{4}{4}$ measure.

Whole note	Half note	Quarter note	Eighth note
o	♩	♩	♪

Whole rest	Half rest	Quarter rest	Eighth rest
▬	▬	𝄽	𝄾

Two eighth notes = One quarter note

♫ = ♩

It is common to join two or more eighth notes with a beam (♫ or ♬). Individual eighth notes look like a quarter note with a flag on the stem (♪ or ♪).

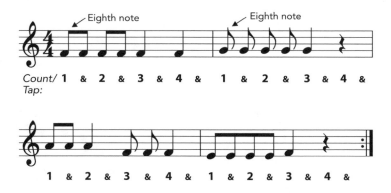

Eighth note   Eighth note

Count/ **1** & **2** & **3** & **4** & **1** & **2** & **3** & **4** &
Tap:

1 & **2** & **3** & **4** & **1** & **2** & **3** & **4** &

Eighth Note Counting

The first eighth note comes on "1" as your foot taps the floor. The second happens as your foot moves up on "&." The third is on "2" and the fourth is on the next "&" and so forth. Remember to count and tap in a steady and even manner, like the ticking of a clock.

Track 25

Skip To My Lou

Keep your fingers close to the keys and curved comfortably.

Track 26

Oh, Susanna

Notice the pick-up notes.

26

William Tell

Good posture will improve your sound.

- Support the clarinet with the thumb of your left hand.
- Curve your fingers so the fleshy part of the finger tip covers all of the tone hole.

Track 28

Two By Two

$\frac{2}{4}$ Time

A time signature of $\frac{2}{4}$ means that a quarter note gets one beat, but there are only two beats in a measure.

Count/ **1 & 2 & 1 & 2 & 1 & 2 & 1 & 2 &**
Tap:

1 & 2 & 1 & 2 & 1 & 2 & 1 & 2 &

Tempo Markings

The speed or pace of music is called **tempo**. Tempo markings are usually written above the staff. Many of these terms come from the Italian.

Allegro *(ah lay' grow)*   Fast tempo

Moderato *(mah der ah' tow)* Medium or moderate tempo

Andante *(ahn dahn' tay)*   Slower "walking" tempo

High School Cadets March

Hey, Ho! Nobody's Home
(New Note: A)

Octaves

Notes that have the same name but are eight notes higher or lower are called **octaves**. You already knew how to play an A, but this new A is one octave lower. Practice playing both A's one after the other like this:

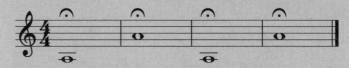

The higher notes will be played more easily if you:

- With your lips, make the air stream round rather than flat.
- Move your jaw slightly forward so the high stream is directed a little higher.
- Blow the air slightly faster.

Track 31

Play The Dynamics

Dynamics

Gradual changes in volume are indicated by these symbols:

      Crescendo (gradually louder) sometimes abbreviated *cresc.*

      Decrescendo or *Diminuendo* (gradually softer) sometimes abbreviated *dim.*

Remember to keep the air stream moving fast both as you get louder by gradually using more air on the crescendo, and as you get softer by gradually using less air on the decrescendo.

Track 32

Frère Jacques

Moderato

Track 33

Hard Rock Blues

Allegro

Posture

Good body posture will allow you to take in a full, deep breath and control the air better as you play. Sit or stand with your spine straight and tall. Your shoulders should be back and relaxed. Think about your posture as you begin playing and check it several times while playing.

Track 34

Alouette

Tie

A *tie* is a curved line connecting two notes of the same pitch. It indicates that instead of playing both notes, you play the first note and hold it for the total time value of both notes.

 = 2 beats

Tie

Dot

A **dot** adds half the value of the note to which it is attached. A dotted half note (♩.) has a total time value of three beats:

Dotted half note   Half note   Quarter note
(three beats)   (two beats)   (one beat)

Therefore, a dotted half note has exactly the same value as a half note tied to a quarter note. Playing track 34 again, compare this music to the previous example:

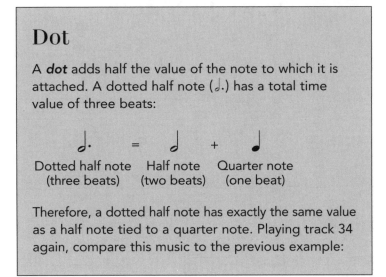

Dot

New Directions (New Note: G)

Track 35

This G is an octave lower than the G you already know. Once again, practice going from one G to the other.

The Nobles

Track 36

Notice the tie across the bar line between the first and second measure. The G on the third beat is held through the following beats 4 and 1.

Track 37

Three Beat Jam

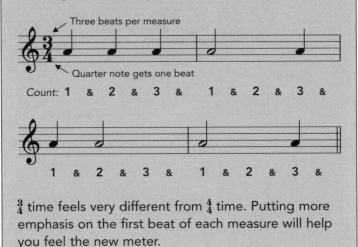

¾ Time

The next song is in ¾ time signature. That is, three beats (quarter notes) per measure.

Three beats per measure

Quarter note gets one beat

Count: **1** & **2** & **3** & **1** & **2** & **3** &

1 & **2** & **3** & **1** & **2** & **3** &

¾ time feels very different from ¼ time. Putting more emphasis on the first beat of each measure will help you feel the new meter.

Morning (from Peer Gynt)

Hand and Finger Position

Now is a good time to go back to page 8 and review proper hand and finger position. This is very important to proper technique. Keeping the fingers curved and close to their assigned keys will allow your fingers and hands to be relaxed and will aid in getting from one note to another quickly, easily, and accurately. The further you lift your fingers off the keys, the more likely that you will put them down on the wrong key or not securely close the key. Besides that, fingers pointing in all directions doesn't look good!

- As you finger the notes on your clarinet, you can practice quietly by speaking the names of the notes, counting out the rhythms, or singing or whistling the pitches.
- Don't let your cheeks puff out when you play.
- Use plenty of air and keep it moving **through** the instrument.

Track 39

Mexican Clapping Song ("Chiapanecas")

Accent

The accent (>) means you should emphasize the note to which it is attached. Do this by using a more explosive "t" on the "tu" with which you produce the note.

Hot Muffins
(New Note: B♭)

Sharps, Flats, and Naturals

Any sharp (♯), flat (♭), or natural (♮) sign that appears in the music but is not in the key signature is called an *accidental*. The accidental in the next example is a B♭ and it effects all of the B's for the rest of the measure.

A **sharp** (♯) raises the pitch of a note by one half step.

A **flat** (♭) lowers the pitch of a note by one half step.

A **natural** (♮) cancels a previous sharp or flat, returning a note to its original pitch.

When a song requires a note to be a half step higher or lower, you'll see a sharp (♯), flat (♭), or natural (♮) sign in front of it. This tells you to raise or lower the note *for that measure only.* We'll see more of these "accidentals" as we continue learning more notes on the clarinet.

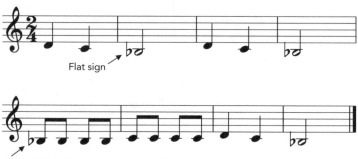

Flat sign

Play all B's in this measure as B♭ (B-flat).

Track 41

Cossack Dance

Notice the repeat sign at the end of the fourth measure. Although this particular repeat sign does not occur at the end of the exercise, it behaves just like any other repeat sign. Play the repeated section twice, then continue.

Track 42

Basic Blues
(New Note: B♭)

Track 43

High Flying

Key Signature – F

The *key signature* tells which notes are played as sharps or flats throughout the entire piece. Until now, all of the exercises have been written in the **Key of C**, which has no sharps or flats. This exercise introduces a new key signature: the **Key of F**. Play B♭ throughout the piece.

1st and 2nd Endings

The use of *1st and 2nd endings* is a variant on the basic repeat sign. You play through the music to the repeat sign and repeat as always, but the second time through the music, skip the measure or measures under the "first ending" and go directly to the "second ending."

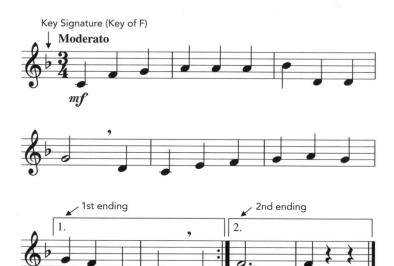

Up On A Housetop

Allegro

Track 45

Waltz Theme

Track 46

Air Time
(New Note: F)

Track 47

Down By The Station

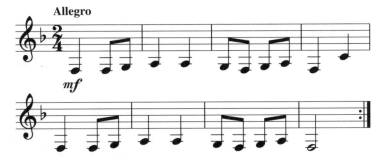

Allegro

Track 48

Banana Boat Song

D.C. al Fine

At the ***D.C. al Fine***, play again from the beginning, stopping at ***Fine***. D.C. is the abbreviation for Da Capo (dah cah' poh), which means "to the beginning." Fine (fee' neh) means "the end."

Always check the key signature.

Moderato

Fine

D.C. al Fine

43

Track 49

Razor's Edge
(New Note: F♯)

Sharp Sign

A sharp sign (♯) raises the pitch of a note by a half-step for the remainder of the measure.

Track 50

The Music Box

Track 51

Smooth Operator

Slur

A curved line connecting notes of different pitch is called a **slur**. Notice the difference between a slur and a tie, which connects notes of the **same** pitch.

Only tongue the first note of a slur. As you finger the next note, keep the breath going. You must precisely change the fingering from one note to the next to prevent extraneous pitches from sounding.

Slur

Gliding Along

Track 52

This exercise is almost identical to the previous one. Notice how the different slurs change the tonguing.

Track 53

Take The Lead

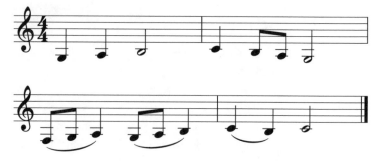

Track 54

The Cold Wind

Phrase

A phrase is a musical "sentence," often 2 or 4 measures long. Try to play a phrase in one breath.

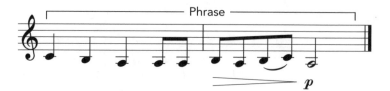

Satin Latin

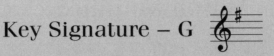

Key Signature – G

A key signature with one sharp indicates that all written F's should be played as F♯'s. This is the **Key of F**.

Multiple Measure Rest

Sometimes you won't play for several measures. The number above the **multiple measure rest** (▬▬) indicates how many full measures to rest. Count through the silent measures.

Two-measure rest

Track 56

March Militaire

Natural Sign

A natural sign (♮) cancels a flat or a sharp for the remainder of the measure.

The Flat Zone
(New Note: E♭)

Check the key signature

On Top Of Old Smokey

Track 59

All Through The Night

Dotted Quarter Note
Remember that a dot adds half the value of the note.
A dotted quarter note followed by a eighth note
(♩. ♪) and (♩‿♪♪) have the same rhythmic value.

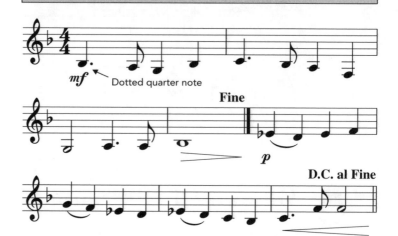

mf Dotted quarter note

Fine

p

D.C. al Fine

Track 60

Sea Chanty

Always use a full air stream.

Moderato

f

mf

f

Scarborough Fair

Auld Lang Syne

Lesson 10

Register key

Notes above the third-line Bb require the *register key* and are called "upper register" notes. Open the register key by rolling your left thumb slightly. Never slide your thumb on and off the key. These high notes will be easier to play if you blow the air faster through your clarinet. If you have trouble, try putting a little more of the mouthpiece in your mouth.

Track 63

Grenadilla Gorilla Jump No. 1
(New Note: E)

Track 64

Grenadilla Gorilla Jump No. 2
(New Note: D)

Grenadilla Gorilla Jump No. 3
(New Note: F)

Grenadilla Gorilla Jump No. 4
(New Note: F♯)

Grenadilla Gorilla Jump No. 5
(New Note: C)

Crossing Over

Alternating between high and low registers is called
crossing the break. You can often save unnecessary
finger movement by leaving the the right-hand fingers
down when you cross the break. This applies only to G
through B♭ in the staff, however.

Right hand down: (4 fingers down) – – – – – – – – – – – – – – – – – –|

(3 fingers down) – – – – – – – – – – –|

Easy Gorilla Jumps
(New Note: G)

German Folk Song

Moderato

mf

1.

2.

Track 71

Michael Row The Boat Ashore

Repeat the section of music enclosed by the repeat signs (‖: ≡ :‖). If 1st and 2nd endings are used, they are played as usual—but go back only to the first repeat sign, not to the beginning.

Track 72

Austrian Waltz

Finlandia

¢ Time Signature

Common time (¢) is the same as $\frac{4}{4}$.

When The Saints Go Marching In

Clarinet Scales and Arpeggios

Key of C

1.

2.

3.

4.

Clarinet Scales and Arpeggios

Key of F

1.

2.

3.

4.

Clarinet Scales and Arpeggios

Key of G

1.

2.

3.

4.

Clarinet Scales and Arpeggios

Key of B♭   Play all B's as B-flat and all E's as E-flat.

Bonus Songs

The last section of this book features five well-known pop and movie favorites. Before we begin, lets review a few things.

Time Signature

The time signature indicates how many beats there are in a measure, and what kind of note gets one beat. $\frac{4}{4}$ is probably the most common time signature. The **top number** tells you how many beats are in each measure; the **bottom number** tells you what kind of note receives one beat. In $\frac{4}{4}$ time there are four beats in the measure and a **quarter note** (♩ or ♪) equals one beat.

Key Signature

Before playing a song always check the **key signature**. A key signature (the group of flats or sharps before the time signature) tells which noyes are played as flats or sharps throughout the entire piece.

Tempo Markings

The speed or pace of music is called **tempo**. Tempo markings are usually written above the staff. Many of these terms come from the Italian.

Allegro	*(ah lay' grow)*	Fast tempo
Moderato	*(mah der ah' tow)*	Medium or moderate tempo
Andante	*(ahn dahn' tay)*	Slower "walking" tempo

Tempo markings can also describe what style to play a piece of music.

Multiple Measure Rest

Sometimes you won't play for several measures. The number above the **multiple measure rest** (▬) indicates how many full measures to rest. Count through the silent measures.

Dynamics

Dynamics refer to how loud or soft the music is. Traditionally, many musical terms (including dynamic markings) are called by their Italian names:

f forte *(four' tay)*   loud

mf mezzo forte *(met' zoh four' tay)* moderately loud

p piano *(pee ahn' oh)*   soft

Gradual changes in volume are indicated by these symbols:

 Crescendo (gradually louder)
sometimes abbreviated *cresc.*

 Decrescendo or *Diminuendo* (gradually softer)
sometimes abbreviated *dim.*

Slur

A curved line connecting notes of different pitch is called a *slur*. Notice the difference between a slur and a tie, which connects notes of the *same* pitch.

Only tongue the first note of a slur. As you finger the next note, keep the breath going. You must precisely change the fingering from one note to the next to prevent extraneous pitches from sounding.

Accent

The accent (>) means you should emphasize the note to which it is attached. Do this by using a more explosive "t" on the "tu" with which you produce the note.

Repeat Signs

Repeat signs tell you to repeat everything between them. If only the sign on the right appears (:‖), repeat from the beginning of the piece.

Fermata

The fermata (⌢) indicates that a note or rest is held somewhat longer than normal.

Now you are ready to play the **bonus songs!**

Forrest Gump – Main Title

(Feather Theme)

from the Paramount Motion Picture FORREST GUMP

Track 75

Music by ALAN SILVESTRI

Copyright © 1994 by Ensign Music Corporation
International Copyright Secured   All Rights Reserved

Track 76

We Will Rock You

Words and Music by BRIAN MAY

© 1977 QUEEN MUSIC LTD.
All Rights Controlled and Administered by BEECHWOOD MUSIC CORP.
All Rights Reserved   International Copyright Secured   Used by Permission

The Man From Snowy River

(Main Title Theme)

from THE MAN FROM SNOWY RIVER

By BRUCE ROWLAND

© 1982 COLGEMS-EMU MUSIC INC. and BRUCE ROWLAND ENTERPRISES PTY. LTD.
Rights for the world excluding Australia, New Zealand and New Guinea
Controlled and Administered by COLGEMS-EMU MUSIC INC.
All Rights Reserved   International Copyright Secured   Used by Permission

Chariots Of Fire

Track 78

from CHARIOTS OF FIRE

Music by VANGELIS

© 1981 EMI MUSIC PUBLISHING LTD.
All Rights for the World, excluding Holland,
Controlled and Administered by EMI APRIL MUSIC INC.
All Rights Reserved   International Copyright Secured   Used by Permission

Rock & Roll – Part II

(The Hey Song)

Words and Music by
MIKE LEANDER and GARY GLITTER

Copyright © 1972 Leeds Music, Ltd.
Copyright Renewed by Palan Music Publishing Ltd. and Songs Of Universal, Inc.
International Copyright Secured   All Rights Reserved

Fingering Chart for Clarinet

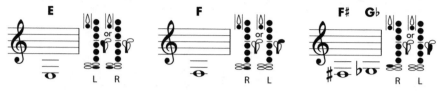

  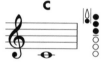

 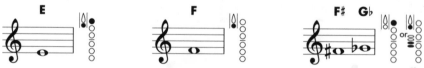 

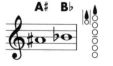 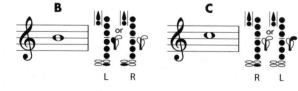

Fingering Chart for Clarinet

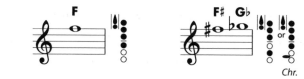

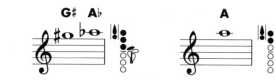

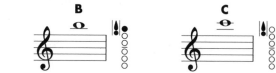

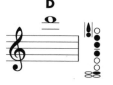

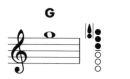
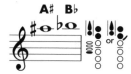

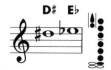

Glossary of Musical Terms

Accent	An Accent mark (>) means you should emphasize the note to which it is attached.
Accidental	Any sharp (♯), flat (♭), or natural (♮) sign that appears in the music but is not in the key signature is called an Accidental.
Allegro	Fast tempo.
Andante	Slower "walking" tempo.
Arpeggio	An Arpeggio is a "broken" chord whose notes are played individually.
Bass Clef (𝄢)	(F Clef) indicates the position of note names on a music staff: The fourth line in Bass Clef is F.
Bar Lines	Bar Lines divide the music staff into measures.
Beat	The Beat is the pulse of music, and like a heartbeat it should remain very steady. Counting aloud and foot-tapping help maintain a steady beat.
Breath Mark	The Breath Mark (,) indicates a specific place to inhale. Play the proceeding note for the full length then take a deep, quick breath through your mouth.
Chord	When two or more notes are played together, they form a Chord or harmony.
Chromatic Notes	Chromatic Notes are altered with sharps, flats and natural signs which are not in the key signature.
Chromatic Scale	The smallest distance between two notes is a half-step, and a scale made up of consecutive half-steps is called a Chromatic Scale.
Common Time	Common Time (𝄴) is the same as $\frac{4}{4}$ time signature.
Crescendo	Play gradually louder. (*cresc.*)
D.C. al Fine	D.C. al Fine means to play again from the beginning, stopping at Fine. D.C. is the abbreviation for Da Capo, or "to the beginning," and Fine means "the end."
Decrescendo	Play gradually softer. (*decresc.*)
Diminuendo	Same as decrescendo. (*dim.*)

Dotted Half Note	A note three beats long in duration (𝅗𝅥.). A dot adds half the value of the note.
Dotted Quarter Note	A note one and a half beats long in duration (♩.). A dot adds half the value of the note.
Double Bar (‖)	Indicates the end of a piece of music.
Duet	A composition with two different parts played together.
Dynamics	Dynamics indicate how loud or soft to play a passage of music. Remember to use full breath support to control your tone at all dynamic levels.
Eighth Note	An Eighth Note (♪) receives half the value of a quarter note, that is, half a beat. Two or more eighth notes are usually joined together with a beam, like this: ♫
Eighth Rest	Indicates 1/2 beat of silence. (𝄾)
Embouchure	Your mouth's position on the mouthpiece of the instrument.
Enharmonics	Two notes that are written differently, but sound the same (and played with the same fingering) are called Enharmonics.
Fermata	The Fermata (𝄐) indicates that a note (or rest) is held somewhat longer than normal.
1st & 2nd Endings	The use of 1st and 2nd Endings is a variant on the basic repeat sign. You play through the music to the repeat sign and repeat as always, but the second time through the music, skip the measure or measures under the "first ending" and go directly to the "second ending."
Flat (♭)	Lowers the note a half step and remains in effect for the entire measure.
Forte (𝆑)	Play loudly.
Half Note	A Half Note (𝅗𝅥) receives two beats. It's equal in length to two quarter notes.
Half Rest	The Half Rest (▬) marks two beats of silence.

Glossary continued

Harmony	Two or more notes played together. Each combination forms a chord.
Interval	The distance between two pitches is an Interval.
Key Signature	A Key Signature (the group of sharps or flats before the time signature) tells which notes are played as sharps or flats throughout the entire piece.
Largo	Play very slow.
Ledger Lines	Ledger Lines extend the music staff. Notes on ledger lines can be above or below the staff.
Mezzo Forte (*mf*)	Play moderately loud.
Mezzo Piano (*mp*)	Play moderately soft.
Moderato	Medium or moderate tempo.
Multiple Measure Rest	The number above the staff tells you how many full measures to rest. Count each measure of rest in sequence. (▬)
Music Staff	The Music Staff has 5 lines and 4 spaces where notes and rests are written.
Natural Sign (♮)	Cancels a flat (♭) or sharp (♯) and remains in effect for the entire measure.
Notes	Notes tell us how high or low to play by their placement on a line or space of the music staff, and how long to play by their shape.
Phrase	A Phrase is a musical "sentence," often 2 or 4 measures long.
Piano (*p*)	Play soft.
Pitch	The highness or lowness of a note which is indicated by the horizontal placement of the note on the music staff.
Pick-Up Notes	One or more notes that come before the first full measure. The beats of Pick-Up Notes are subtracted from the last measure.
Quarter Note	A Quarter Note (♩) receives one beat. There are 4 quarter notes in a $\frac{4}{4}$ measure.

Quarter Rest	The Quarter Rest (𝄽) marks one beat of silence.
Repeat Sign	The Repeat Sign (:𝄂) means to play once again from the beginning without pause. Repeat the section of music enclosed by the repeat signs (𝄆 ≡ :𝄂). If 1st and 2nd endings are used, they are played as usual—but go back only to the first repeat sign, not to the beginning.
Rests	Rests tell us to count silent beats.
Rhythm	Rhythm refers to how long, or for how many beats a note lasts.
Scale	A Scale is a sequence of notes in ascending or descending order. Like a musical "ladder," each step is the next consecutive note in the key signature.
Sharp (♯)	Raises the note a half step and remains in effect for the entire measure.
Slur	A curved line connecting notes of different pitch is called a Slur.
Tempo	Tempo is the speed of music.
Tempo Markings	Tempo Markings are usually written above the staff, in Italian. (Allegro, Moderato, Andante)
Tie	A Tie is a curved line connecting two notes of the same pitch. It indicates that instead of playing both notes, you play the first note and hold it for the total time value of both notes.
Time Signature	Indicates how many beats per measure and what kind of note gets one beat.
Treble Clef (𝄞)	(G Clef) indicates the position of note names on a music staff: The second line in Treble Clef is G.
Trio	A Trio is a composition with three parts played together.
Whole Note	A Whole Note (𝅝) lasts for four full beats (a complete measure in $\frac{4}{4}$ time).
Whole Rest	The Whole Rest (𝄻) indicates a whole measure of silence.